A PANEGYRIC ON APOLLO
ARCHIMANDRITE OF THE MONASTERY OF ISAAC
BY STEPHEN
BISHOP OF HERACLEOPOLIS MAGNA

INTRODUCTION

This Coptic Panegyric on Apollo, Archimandrite of the Monastery of Isaac, is contained in a Pierpont Morgan manuscript, M 579, fols. 130v-148r. It is attributed to Stephen, Bishop of Heracleopolis Magna. Nothing is known about the author, except that he was a monk at the Monastery of Isaac before he became a bishop. The manuscript from which the text is taken is dated in a colophon in A.D. 822-823. The events narrated in the panegyric lead us back into the sixth century, more precisely into the reign of Justinian I (A.D. 527-565). The date of the work cannot be determined with any certainty, but it may be conjectured that it was written by A.D. 600 or thereabouts.

The panegyric recounts episodes from the life of Apollo and extols his virtues and his spiritual prowess. As is customary in such eulogies, miracles are attributed to the hero. In the present work, some of these are conventional and modelled on stories from the Old and New Testaments, while others are highly original. But it is the references to historical events of the period which give a very special interest to the work. At that time, hostility erupted once more between the adherents of Chalcedon and the Monophysites. These struggles are reflected in the work. There is also an important reference to the existence of a Meletian community. In addition to many biblical references the panegyric also contains some patristic quotations[1].

In arrangement, the English translation follows the edition of the Coptic text. Words in round brackets, unless stated otherwise, have no equivalent in the Coptic and have been added to provide an idiomatic English translation. All references to the Old Testament in the footnotes are to the Septuagint.

---

[1] The problem of authorship and date is discussed more fully in the volume containing the edition of the Coptic text where there is also a more extensive analysis of the contents.

1. A panegyric delivered by our God-loving holy father, in every way honoured and perfect in the knowledge of the scriptures inspired by God[1], Apa Stephen, the Bishop of the city of Hnēs[2], in honour of our holy father, the prophet and archimandrite, Apa Apollo of the
5 Monastery of Isaac. While he was still a monk in this same monastery, before he became a bishop, he delivered this panegyric to the glory of our Lord Jesus Christ and his servant the prophet, our holy father Apa Apollo, who completed his honoured course[3] on the 20th of the month Paōne[4]. In the peace of God. Amen.
10 2. There has risen for us today like a great light from heaven the day of repose of our holy father the prophet Apa Apollo who truly enjoyed God according to the symphony of his name[5]. For I, said God, am the Alpha and the Omega[6]. Our father, therefore, began in God and the perfecter, too, was God. So now it was well said
15 by Solomon: The memory of the just is a good report[7]. For truly, O our father, your memorial has been as the wine of Lebanon[8], as it is written, and the sweet odour of your sufferings has been spread abroad. For which are the villages and lands from which no one has gathered here today to come and worship and enjoy Christ our
20 Lord who is upon the mystic table instead of the manger of Bethlehem? In fitting manner, therefore, I shall raise my voice with the psalmist: The Lord * gathered them out of their lands[9], he led them   * p. 2
in a straight way (that they might go up to)[10] the city of habitation[11] of his saint who became founder and originator of this monastery
25 after Christ; he who also is gathered with us today with his angelic host as he promised in the holy gospels[12]. How exceedingly great

---

[1] Cf. II *Tim.* 3.*16.*

[2] I.e. Heracleopolis Magna. The city is referred to in *Is.* 30.*4* as חֲנֵס.

[3] Cf. *Acts* 13.*25*, 20.*24.*

[4] I.e. 14th June.

[5] The play on words in the text based on the similarity of sound between the name ⲁⲡⲟⲗⲗⲱ and the verb ⲁⲡⲟⲗⲁⲩⲉ cannot be imitated in English.

[6] *Rev.* 1.*8*, 21.*6*, 22.*13.*

[7] *Prov.* 10.*7.*

[8] Cf. *Hos.* 14.*8.*

[9] Cf. *Ps.* 106.*3.*

[10] The bracketed words which occur in *Ps.* 106.7 have probably been omitted in error in the text.

[11] Cf. *Ps.* 106.*7.*

[12] Cf. *Mt.* 18.*20.*

is the company upon earth from among those in heaven! And since
you, too, have come to us because of this, O Christ-loving people, at
the call of my Saviour, we do not wish to send you away hungry in
spirit, lest you faint in the way of virtue in which you walk[13]. But
through my Saviour's unlimited bounty I wish to prepare a poor   5
repast for you with the honours of our father, not as if I were fit for
this, but because the honouring of the fathers is an obligation in the
law and the gospel, especially so good a father whose comeliness has
been exalted above the heavens. Therefore I shall spread before you
a spiritual table of his honourable life, for I know that the works of 10
the righteous bring forth life for those who follow him, as it is written[14].
On this same spiritual table, therefore, which is the life of our father,
you will find the faith and obedience of the patriarchs towards God,
the meekness and lack of vindictiveness of Moses and David, the
tranquillity of Joshua (the son of)[15] Nun, the purity of the great 15
* p. 3 Elijah and * his zeal against those who provoke God to jealousy; in
sum, the suffering of the prophets, the renunciation of the apostles,
the steadfastness in struggles that are no less than those of the
martyrs. If you are at a loss whence a spiritual and fruit-bearing
tree such as this sprang up, mark and consider within yourself the 20
life of this man like that of the apostles.

3. Now this man was created in the image of God[16] and he kept
the honour of the image pure. Then after the feeding with milk (and)
after the increase in stature (and) after the time when the cockerel
crows, that is after the discerning man's reason came to him, then 25
he no longer followed after flesh and blood, nor did he walk in
the life of the things of this world, but he adopted the example of
the patriarch Abraham who came out from his country and his
kindred and his father's house[17] into the land flowing with milk
and honey[18], I am referring to the holy community of Pbow, even if 30
that true vine which was formerly beloved has now turned to bitter-
ness[19]. But as for the patriarch, even though he forsook his country,
yet all his belongings remained with him, as the holy scripture testi-

---

[13] Cf. *Mt. 15.32.*
[14] Cf. *Prov. 10.16.*
[15] The bracketed words have probably been omitted in error in the text.
[16] Cf. *Gen. 1.27.*
[17] Cf. *Gen. 12.1.*
[18] Cf. *Ex. 3.8* etc.
[19] Cf. *Jer. 2.21.*

CORPUS

SCRIPTORUM CHRISTIANORUM ORIENTALIUM

EDITUM CONSILIO

UNIVERSITATIS CATHOLICAE AMERICAE

ET UNIVERSITATIS CATHOLICAE LOVANIENSIS

Vol. 395

SCRIPTORES COPTICI

TOMUS 40

A PANEGYRIC ON APOLLO
Archimandrite of the Monastery of Isaac
BY STEPHEN
Bishop of Heracleopolis Magna

TRANSLATED

BY

K. H. KUHN

LOUVAIN
Secrétariat du CorpusSCO
Waversebaan, 49
1978

ISBN 2 8017 0088 6

D/1978/0602/11

Imprimerie Orientaliste, s.p.r.l., Louvain (Belgique)

fies²⁰. This man, on the other hand, let virtue be for him instead
of all his belongings. Abraham was obedient to God and offered
up to him as sacrifice his beloved son in accordance with the purpose
of his heart²¹. But this man presented himself a living sacrifice, holy,
5 well-pleasing to God²². Abraham walked * for three days on the road   * p. 4
up to the mountain of his sacrifice²³. But this man endured over
so great a distance from this district until he went up to the monastery
established on the mountain. I am referring to the life of our holy
fathers Apa Pachomius, the first and greatest among the archimandrites,
10 and to the heir both of his suffering and of his virtue who was appointed
and was first to give himself as a gift to God; I am referring to
Theodore²⁴ who was united in soul with the former, and to his
fellow-worker in the Lord who was Horsiesios. Now when he who
was at that time successor in the ministry of these men saw the holy
15 Apa Apollo, he knew by the piety of his manner and the strictness
of his habits that he was an honoured vessel, pleasing to the Lord and
ready for every good work. He then received him with honour²⁵
and, as it is further written, held him by his right hand²⁶, took him
into his holy monastery and girded him with the armour of righteous-
20 ness²⁷; I am referring to the holy monastic habit. This is a very inferior
thing by reason of its appearance, yet its power reaches to the sceptre-
bearing²⁸ spirits. He was clothed with the tunic that by this the
remembrance of leaving this life should become for him a subject
for meditation. For we wear such a garment physically when we are
25 leaving this dwelling-place, although we give it again to the earth
with the earth, which is our wretched body. But in my view, I say
that it has denoted the cleanness or purity of the body, for our
linen is a pure material, as * it were a plant on the earth, and not   * p. 5
the result of procreation. And did not God command through the

---

²⁰ Cf. *Gen.* 12.5.
²¹ Cf. *Gen.* 22.1 ff.
²² Cf. *Rom.* 12.1.
²³ Cf. *Gen.* 22.4.
²⁴ Possibly a play on words on the name Theodore (ΘΕΟΛΩΡΟC) is intended in
the reference to the "gift (ΛΩΡΟΝ) to (of) God".
²⁵ Cf. *Ps.* 72.24.
²⁶ Cf. *Ps.* 72.23.
²⁷ Cf. II *Cor.* 6.7.
²⁸ The Greek word in the Coptic text is corrupt. The translation assumes that it
stands for σκηπτροκράτωρ.

priestly prophet Ezekiel[29] in the Old Testament that they should
gird themselves with linen breeches before they go in to minister[30]?
   4. After the tunic he was clothed with a sheepskin cloak fashioned
according to the precept of the angels, denoting again what I said
before, namely the death of the body, that through this he should   5
become dead to all fleshly desires. They put upon him a hood as on a
child[31] according to the grace of the holy calling. For a child is
not only small in stature but is also innocent and guileless. For thus
the Saviour called the apostles after the resurrection 'children'[32],
although this was not their bodily state. He was girded with a girdle   10
as with the habit of Elijah and John[33], the forerunners, that by this
also he should become strong against the pleasures of the belly and
those below the belly[34]. For whoso has not the things which the
ascetic life requires but carries only the staff of piety, yet denies its
power, they, I say, are like whitewashed sepulchres[35] and soulless   15
gravestones, those who have the name of the living or of those who
have lived but are lifeless. So I have spoken, though I myself am poor
and also despised, but the perfect lawgiver and model of all virtue, Apa
Shenoute, said of him who prays, whose mind is only a stick or
who is distracted by things unfitting : He is worse than an idol, since   20
this, he said, does not think of any evil for it is soulless, * but that one
has misused his intellect[36]. But our father is not such a one, the son
of the apostles is not such a one. But as if he had girded himself
with power for war, he thereafter pursued his enemies and did not
turn back until he had destroyed them. Moreover, like those who   25
run in the race[37], who go on pursuing (the things of) the belly, and
do not stop at all until they reach the place where the prizes are, so
is this blessed man who runs dutifully at all times in the race of virtue.
And in this he resembles the progress of the incorporeal powers, who
are the chariot-bearers of the Lord, whom the prophet Ezekiel saw   30

* p. 6

---

[29] Cf. *Ez.* 1.3.
[30] Cf. *Ez.* 44.18.
[31] The wearing of the hood (ⲕⲟⲩⲕⲣⲓⲟⲛ - κουκούλλιον) by children and monks alike
encouraged speculation on its symbolic meaning. For examples from patristic literature,
see G. W. H. LAMPE, *A Patristic Greek Lexicon* (Oxford, 1968), p. 773a.
[32] *John* 21.5.
[33] I.e. John the Baptist.
[34] I.e. sexual pleasures.
[35] Cf. *Mt.* 23.27.
[36] I cannot identify the quotation attributed to Shenoute.
[37] Cf. I *Cor.* 9.24.

going without turning backwards at all, not even with their faces[38].
For such a one is he in his race, as he goes forward daily in the prac-
tice of asceticism and comes to increase in virtue. And as having
been built upon the foundation of the apostles and prophets[39], he
5 built himself up as a spiritual house[40] of God with precious stones,
which are the fruits of the Holy Spirit[41] : a pure converse in his mind
with God; a lifting up of his holy hands[42], which are the vanquishers
of the spiritual Amalekites[43]; meditation proof against distraction,
for through this he became a shooter of sharp arrows into the heart(s)
10 of the enemies of Christ the king; fellowship with the elect; renunciation of his desires; asceticism full of discernment; disciplining of the
belly and the pleasures which arise from surfeiting it; a reconciliation
of the flesh to the spirit through the unity of virtue, but especially
the exercise of the diversity * of these severally which is the sum of all   * p. 7
15 philosophy. For this man's nourishment is the enjoyment of holy
words, and his whole pleasure is the remembrance of God. This man's
pride is the fear of the Lord[44], and his whole desire is his law[45].

5. But why do I attempt to count the multitude of the stars? I am
speaking of the abundance of the virtuous actions of this blessed
20 man who is worthy of heaven. For who, O our father, has preserved
perfection like you, O our father, with the likeness of God in him
undefiled? Who has achieved the impassibility of the incorporeal beings
more than you while yet in the body? What earthborn man has
trodden under the nature of those on earth and has acquired the
25 nobility of those in heaven that he might be with them like you, O
our father? O, how shall I be able to speak of the greatness of the
honours which befit this holy man, man in his nature but equal to the
angels in his ways, this earth-born man according to his substance
but son of God and brother of Christ according to his way of life!
30 For he who shall do, he said, the will of my Father who is in heaven,

---

[38] Cf. *Ez.* 1.9, *17*; 10.*11*.
[39] Cf. *Eph.* 2.20.
[40] Cf. I *Pet.* 2.5.
[41] Cf. *Gal.* 5.22.
[42] Cf. I *Tim.* 2.8 etc.
[43] The Amalekites of the O.T. are the arch-enemy of the people of Israel. They
are defeated by Moses holding up his hands (cf. *Ex.* 17.8ff.). Their spiritual counter-
part is, it may be conjectured, sin which is defeated by prayer.
[44] Cf. *Ecclus.* 10.22.
[45] Cf. *Ps.* 1.2.

he is my brother and my sister and my mother[46]. But so that I may summarize for you the whole in a few (words): he took up his cross and followed the Lord[47]. And he ascended on high with him[48], and he did not descend until his end, as neither did his Lord. For truly the ascent to the cross is that man is on high with the eternal 5 in his thought and that he crucifies the flesh and the desires[49]. For thus said the apostle: I have been crucified with Christ[50]. Never-
* p. 8 theless, * after he had ascended on high so completely and after he had become such a spiritual house[51], he also kept the observance of the legislation of Deuteronomy which commands him who would construct 10 such a house for himself to surround his roof with a parapet lest anyone fall from it[52], which is humility, the fullness and guardian of every virtue at all times. Therefore he was greatly exalted according to the promise of our Saviour[53]. Because of this or through this, he, having been exalted, flourished in the house of God. Through this the 15 glory of the Lord shone upon him. Because of this the riches of the grace[54] of the Holy Spirit justly rested upon him, perfect prophecy, wonderful visions with[55] workings of miracles[56], gifts of healing[57], authority over the demons to cast them out[58]. But so that you should not doubt when you hear these things, I shall curb your insensibility 20 by what I shall first set forth as proof of what I have said. I shall make you see him contend with the spirits of wickedness; afterwards he receives the crown from the judge of these aforesaid contests, our Lord, our Saviour. I shall bring him to you by remembering him as he sweated because of the exercise of virtues, that you may not doubt 25 when you see him sitting down beside the King of heaven after his coming out from the arena of this life. I shall make known to you a portion of his toils and his virtues which he accomplished, that you

[46] *Mt. 12.50.*
[47] Cf. *Mt. 16.24* etc.
[48] Cf. perhaps *Eph. 4.8* (*Ps. 67.19*).
[49] Cf. *Gal. 5.24.*
[50] *Gal. 2.19.*
[51] Cf. I *Pet. 2.5.*
[52] Cf. *Deut. 22.8.*
[53] Cf. *Mt. 23.12*; *Lk. 14.11, 18.14.*
[54] Cf. perhaps *Eph. 1.7* etc.
[55] Possibly omit ϩⲛ- "with".
[56] Cf. I *Cor. 12.10.*
[57] Cf. I *Cor. 12.9.*
[58] Cf. *Mk. 3.15.*

may not disbelieve when you see him enjoy * the fruits of his toils. * p. 9
For the honours belong to those who have toiled and the crowns
to those who have overcome, according to the word of the great Basil[59].
For this the imitator of Christ, the wise apostle, also did, who first
5 put down his perils and his many fastings and his vigils and the care
for the churches[60] and (about) the government which apprehended
him in Damascus[61] before he told of his being caught up into
Paradise and the revelation of hidden words[62] and the exhortation
of God which came to him as a consolation in his illness[63].

10   6. So then our father, too, who is the object of this gathering
today, worthy to be loved, chose for himself wisdom from his youth on.
Therefore he became holy in his hands (and) pure in his heart, that
means in deed and thought, until his end, for he appeared perfect in
both parts. For the one, which is the body, he devoted to the exercise
15 of the toils of virtue, but the soul he kept pure for spiritual contem-
plation. For those who know have testified concerning him that carnal
pleasure was never in him, either through the help of the Most High
overshadowing him, or through his curbing the body effectively, the
constitution of which lies in the four elements of the world[64]. For
20 it was said concerning our father the prophet, Apa Apollo, that in the
beginning, * when he went to Pbow, he devoted himself to many vigils, *p. 10
so that he spent three years without ever lying down to sleep during
the whole night and day. And if he wished to give way to refreshing
sleep for a little, he would do this for a brief moment, squatting
25 on his toes, that the natural sweetness of sleep should not beguile him.
So therefore spiritual comfort rightly flourished for him in this kind
of contest. For many times after the end of the day, night would fall
and he would see angelic choirs and ranks of prophets coming to him
and transporting him to their glory and making him more than eager
30 for virtue by reciting to him their feats of prowess in which they

---

[59] This is a quotation from the Prooemium in regulas fusius tractatas, see MIGNE,
Patrologia graeca 31, 892C; for a Coptic version of the passage, see the unedited
manuscript in the John Rylands Library, Manchester, Ryl. 62, fol. 3r.
[60] Cf. II *Cor.* 11.26-28.
[61] Cf. II *Cor.* 11.32.
[62] Cf. II *Cor.* 12.4.
[63] Cf. II *Cor.* 12.9.
[64] The wording is perhaps somewhat reminiscent of *Wisd.* 7.17. The idea itself is
well documented in antiquity, cf. G. KITTEL, *Theologisches Wörterbuch zum Neuen
Testament* VII, pp. 672ff. Note especially the definition of στοιχεῖα by the Alexandrian
lexicographer Hesychius (5th century A.D.): πῦρ, ὕδωρ, γῆ καὶ ἀήρ, ἀφ ὧν τὰ σώματα.

themselves had been previously engaged. Now Isaiah said to him
thus : I spent the whole time of my career as a prophet wearing sackcloth
and even this was not allowed to me, but another three years were
allotted for me to be naked[65]. And the end[66] of my sufferings came
to me at last through my being sawn asunder contrary to the law of   5
human kindness[67]. But Jeremiah answered : I, too, was not allowed
even the earth to walk on, but I was made to sit in a pit of mire[68]. I was
put into the stocks[69], and my death came to me by stoning[70].
Ezekiel also said to him : But as for me, even the rest of sleep which
belongs to all nature I made into a chastisement for myself[71], and   10
* p. 11   my food was * in very short supply for me[72]. And because of my severity
with regard to the word of truth, the slaying with the sword by my kins-
men came upon me[73]. So in brief, each one of the saints would speak
to him of his contests, making him through these exceedingly zealous
in virtue.   15

7. But do not doubt, O listener, when you hear these things. For
if the patriarch Jacob saw the army of God and the angels of God
met him[74] before the archetypal law[75], how much more is it fitting
that this man — I am referring to our father — should become more
fully son and minister of the grace of the gospel. Take also John   20
Chrysostom who says as follows : As the birds that fly aloft, when
they look down on the earth and see on a green patch their fellows
of the same species as themselves, slacken (their flight) and come
down and alight by them, so do the angels, when they see those who
have chosen for themselves purity in temptations, come quickly and   25

---

[65] Cf. *Is.* 20.2-3.

[66] Or possibly : "flowering".

[67] Cf. *Asc. Is.* 5.11-14, and also Lives of the Prophets 13 (ed. P. RIESSLER, *Alt-jüdisches Schrifttum ausserhalb der Bibel* (Heidelberg, 1966), p. 874).

[68] Cf. *Jer.* 45.6.

[69] Cf. *Jer.* 20.2.

[70] According to Jewish legend, Jeremiah was stoned to death by his compatriots in Egypt, cf. W. RUDOLPH, *Jeremia*, Handbuch zum Alten Testament 12 (Tübingen, 1958), pp. VII-VIII; cf. also Lives of the Prophets 14 (ed. RIESSLER, *op. cit.*, p. 875).

[71] Cf. *Ez.* 4.4-8.

[72] Cf. *Ez.* 4.9ff.

[73] Cf. Lives of the Prophets 15 (ed. RIESSLER, *op. cit.*, p. 876).

[74] Cf. *Gen.* 32.1.

[75] The precise meaning of the reference to the archetypal law escapes me. Does it mean that the law of Moses had not yet been promulgated when the vision of the angels was vouchsafed to Jacob, and that this law prefigures the greater law of Jesus, the gospel?

help their fellows[76]. But why do I bring forward these things and others as I have the voice of my Saviour confirming this to us? For as for him who will keep my word, he said, I shall come with my Father and we shall make for ourselves an abode with him[77],

5 who therefore became a holy temple of the Lord[78] — I am referring to our father. Why do you doubt concerning the meeting with him of the species of incorporeal beings? If[79] you have taken root in the faith of the things which you hear, then, after the saints, I shall extend to you the vision of the Lord of the saints. * For it once so happened,   * p. 12

10 they said, that this saint, our father Apa Apollo, was in the harvest with the brethren, fasting as was his custom. For many times he would not eat for two days running, and oftentimes he would spend the whole week fasting, observing a fast in this way and harvesting with the brethren. Suffering bore heavily upon him and as a result

15 of the great suffering he drew apart and sat down. And so an ecstasy fell upon him. And in the ecstasy a wonderful vision appeared to him. He saw the Lord standing beside him after the fashion in which he was lifted up upon the cross with that awestruck company which was round about the holy cross. So then the Lord spoke to him : Apollo, have

20 you suffered as I, or have you submitted to a part of the things that were done to me? And at once the saint awoke and the strength of the Lord dwelt with him from that day onwards. For those who submit to God shall be transformed in their strength[80]. Furthermore, they shall go from strength to strength[81], from human weakness to the

25 power of the Lord. Therefore, inasmuch as he had received such grace from the Lord, he devoted himself to highly exalted contests and to struggles with the spirits of evil[82]. For it was testified about him that often at baking time, when the ovens were left at the evening baking, he would go there while they were still hot and stand upon them and

30 pray until morning, remembering the struggle of the three holy children[83], so that the ground under him became like mud because of the greatness of the heat and the amount of sweat that came down

---

[76] I cannot identify the quotation attributed to John Chrysostom.
[77] Cf. *John* 14.23.
[78] Cf. *Eph.* 2.21.
[79] This translation assumes that ⲉⲕⲝⲉ stands for ⲉⲱⲝⲉ.
[80] *Is. 40.31.*
[81] *Ps. 83.8.*
[82] Cf. *Eph. 6.12.*
[83] Cf. *Dan. 3.16* ff.

* p. 13 on it. But in the days of winter * he would do the opposite. For the
garment which he wore he would soak with water and put on and
stand in frost and dew all through the night praying. Sometimes also
he would go down to places filled with water and stand in them so
that the pain of the freezing water should banish the sensation of sleep.   5
    8. O you who hear this, do then such contests as these seem to you
inferior to those of the martyrs? Rather, if it is right that the truth
be proclaimed, there are many among the holy martyrs whose whole
contest lasted only for a brief hour or a single day, but this man
was dying almost daily[84] by ascetic sufferings. And since such contests   10
are not inferior to those of the martyrs, listen to the great Basil when
he says about the way of life which is asceticism: All the saints
lived in it and became martyrs through it[85]. Also the apostolic Athanasius, the chosen, testifies concerning the great Antony: He was a
martyr daily in his conscience[86]. For the sufferings of the holy way of   15
life are called with one accord: martyrdoms. But do not be perplexed
when you hear this, for behold I have made known to you the power
of God whose power is manifest in the weakness of nature[87], as he
said to his chosen one, Paul. Then while the saint and truly beloved
of God, our father Apa Apollo, still was in these (sufferings) and while   20
these (sufferings) still were in him, and while he was still as an olive
tree in fruit in the house of God, and while all the air was yet pure,
suddenly the sky became thick with clouds. Great hail rained from on
* p. 14 high upon men[88], not according to virtues' desert. * Then the lion that
had been hidden came forth from his lair to seize someone. I saw,   25
said John in his Apocalypse, a star that had fallen from heaven. The
pit of the abyss was opened. Smoke of a great fire went up. The
sun and the air became dark through the smoke of the pit[89], the
pit of the impiety which the rulers had gathered up who had come
together to Chalcedon. This very pit of the abyss was opened again   30

---

[84] Cf. perhaps I *Cor. 15.31.*
[85] I cannot identify the quotation attributed to Basil of Caesarea.
[86] See *The Life of St. Antony,* ed. MIGNE, *Patrologia graeca* 26, 912B. Cf. ed. G.
GARITTE, *S. Antonii vitae versio sahidica,* C.S.C.O. 117/Copt. 13 (Louvain, 1949), p. 110,
col. II, lines 18-20, cf. also p. 53, lines 25-26; for a Latin translation, see *op. cit.,* C.S.C.O.
118/*Copt. 14* (Louvain, 1949), p. 60, lines 22-23, cf. also p. 29, line 31.
[87] Cf. II *Cor. 12.9.*
[88] Cf. *Rev. 16.21.*
[89] Cf. *Rev. 9.1-2.*

in the days of the Emperor Justinian[90]. Again that soul-destroying
madness, again the torrents of lawlessness flowed in their ravines
to shake[91] the house of the faithful. For after Marcian[92], the originator of the innovation[93] of the faith, had finished, and after Basiliscus[94]
5 and Zeno[95] and still others after these, the bad weed grew again
in the kingdom of Justinian like a hidden fire in chaff which continues
to produce smoke.

9. Now the wretched bishops who had come together at Chalcedon became food for perdition and death and error, but their sins
10 continue to be active. And their wickedness was unending and their
punishment also is unceasing. For the fire of apostasy which those
wretched bishops kindled everywhere drew to itself the laments and
tears of the holy prophets unto the end. For let the pine tree weep,
said the prophet Zechariah, because the cedar has fallen[96]. This means :
15 Let the people * weep, for their bishops have fallen in a fall deliberately   * p. 15
chosen, that is of their deliberate choice. Jeremiah also laments over
them, saying : Many shepherds have destroyed my vineyard[97]. I shall
yet again adduce another third prophetic lament, for their impiety
is against the Trinity. Woe to the peoples, said Nahum, for their
20 shepherds have slumbered in spirit. The king of the Assyrians who
is hidden[98] has laid to rest a ruler[99], for the rulers of the church are
the bishops, as the holy apostles said. There is no healing, he[100] said,
for their ruin[101]. For what healing shall come to them, who have
rejected the chief physician of our nature, the Lord of glory, the Word
25 of the Father, the only begotten Son of God? He it is who took upon
himself according to the dispensation full of the love towards men our

---

[90] Justinian I reigned A.D. 527-565.
[91] The translation assumes that ноι stands for Coptic ноєιν.
[92] Marcian (with Pulcheria) reigned A.D. 450-457.
[93] κενοдομιλ probably stands for καινοτομία. Alternatively, the spelling may
indicate that the noun should be derived from κενοτομέω which was used as pun on
καινοτομέω (cf. G.W.H. LAMPE, A Patristic Greek Lexicon, p. 743a), "empty innovation".
[94] Basiliscus, the usurper, reigned A.D. 475-477.
[95] Zeno reigned A.D. 474-491.
[96] Zech. 11.2.
[97] Jer. 12.10.
[98] I.e. unrevealed, perhaps to be understood as a cipher for the devil.
[99] Perhaps read : "their rulers".
[100] I.e. Nahum.
[101] Cf. Nahum 3.18-19.

nature, which is the holy flesh of natural beings, rational, and spiritual, which he received through the Holy Spirit from our glorious Lady, the God-bearing holy Virgin Mary. He also made her one with himself according to his substance[102], for he is not divided into two natures[103], God forbid, or two persons[104] as it seemed good to 5 the foul council, but he is one Lord, one Christ, one and the same without change and division, whether at the time when he performs the highest wonders or at the time when he endures the physical sufferings in which there is no discredit, being in them all in every way undivided and unchanging. But those of the Council of Chalcedon 10 renounced this apostolic doctrine and true teaching of all the teachers of truth, and they divided according to the thought of the Jews' religion this single one, our Lord Jesus Christ, into two natures and two

* p. 16 persons, and instead of the holy Trinity * they advanced an unlawful quaternity. Therefore, according to the word of the prophet, there is no 15 healing for the ruin that overtook them[105]. I shall bring forward again, as it is fitting, the words of the prophet. He said with regard to this council : All that hear news of you shall clap their hands over you; for upon whom has not your wickedness come all the time[106]?

10. For indeed it was not only the apostolic throne of Alexandria 20 which displayed its light, the holy Dioscorus[107], set at that time by Christ upon the high-priestly lampstand, but (so did) almost the whole country of Egypt and in addition also the holy community of Pbow, which was reached by the aforementioned tempest not only in former times but also in the days of the Emperor Justinian. And who will 25 be able to see, or who will be able to hear the misery of the orthodox at that time? For the pillar of orthodoxy and the veritable athlete of election, the holy Severus, the holy patriarch of Antioch[108], devoted himself to many journeyings while being watched over, though much more by God, as herald of orthodoxy. The emperor called also the 30 patriarch of Alexandria, our father Theodosius[109], to him to Constantinople, outwardly as if honouring his priesthood, but actually he

---

[102] ὑπόστασις.
[103] φύσις.
[104] πρόσωπον.
[105] Cf. Nahum 3.19.
[106] Nahum 3.19.
[107] A.D. 444-451.
[108] A.D. 512-518 (died A.D. 538).
[109] A.D. 535-536 (died A.D. 566).

wanted to detain him with him in order that his ordination should
be invalidated. I shall stop up, said that emperor, * these great rivers, * p. 17
that their canals and their backwaters may dry up. I shall hide, he
said, the light under the bushel[110], that the feet of those who run to it
5 shall stumble. What lament then is not for the orthodox at that
time? The churches were desolate, your[111] clerics were few. The
majority of the orthodox bishops had fallen asleep in the faith, being
perfect in the teaching of their father. Thus then when the darkness
of the error had spread abroad, the wild beasts spoke out boldy,
10 wolf upon wolf, to advance towards the sheep of the Lord. They who
came together at Chalcedon mixed the cup[112] of the Jews' religion,
and he who shall drink it, his reward is the office of archimandrite of
Pbow. O wicked demand, O bitter conflict! The command came, the
wolf advanced, the emperor's edict went forth. And as it is written,
15 that emperor sent forth his darts[113]. He troubled the brethren of the
holy community. He multiplied his threats to scatter the sheep of the
Lord, if they did not want to transgress the faith of the Lord. In this
then were revealed the fountains of spiritual water, that is this holy
community and the other congregations which Christ established at
20 that time. But in what way? Great is the history, however of necessity
we shall tell it through others. For when the holy brethren saw that
their faithful shepherd, the latter-day patriarch, Abraham[114], who
was archimandrite at that time, was taken away from them, and
that the transgressor whom the emperor had sent was appointed to
25 stand in the place of this man, all who loved godliness acted * with * p. 18
great zeal and chose to leave the dwelling-place of their fathers lest
they should make themselves strangers to the God of their fathers.
The affair extended to distant paths, O my beloved, but by going
through the thorns they find the lily. For our holy father Apa Apollo
30 is in truth a lily who uprooted himself from among the thorns of
the heretics. And thus he departed from Pbow at that time, having
kept as apostolic the Constitution of the Apostles which says: If the

[110] Cf. perhaps *Mt*. 5.15; *Mk*. 4.21; *Lk*. 11.33.
[111] Perhaps read: "the".
[112] Cf. perhaps *Rev*. 18.6.
[113] Cf. II *Kg*. 22.15 etc.
[114] Cf. P. VAN CAUWENBERGH, *Étude sur les moines d'Égypte depuis le Concile de Chalcédoine (451) jusqu'à l'invasion arabe (640)* (Paris-Louvain, 1914), pp. 154ff.; A. GRILLMEIER and H. BACHT, *Das Konzil von Chalkedon* II (Würzburg, 1953), pp. 334f.

ungodly seize a monastery[115], flee far away. For it is not the place that commends man, but it is man who commends the place[116]. For thus the three holy children who were in the fiery furnace in Babylon called God to them by their steadfastness[117]. But as for the Jews, while they still possessed the temple as their sanctuary, this only 5 begotten Son of God departed from their midst because of their hypocrisy. As one taught by God, thus did our father take upon himself the retreat (from the world), wandering in the deserts and ravines and holes of the earth[118], being a sojourner in an alien region, in want, distressed, and grieved[119]. After all this it was as if he heard 10 from God what he had said to the patriarch Jacob : Return to the land in which you were born and I shall do good unto you[120]. And after many wanderings he came to this very mountain. And only when * p. 19 he stood on it, * he heard Isaiah saying : God shall give rest upon this mountain[121], and also David : This is the mountain which God 15 desired and he lived in it[122]. As is fitting he, too, said : This is my dwelling-place for ever. I shall live in it[123], for the Lord has chosen it as a monastery for himself.

11. These are the good deeds of our father before (attaining) the dignity of father. These are the contests in which he shone while yet 20 in the ranks of the army of the spirit before he became a commander. It was these things which summoned him justly through the Saviour to the spiritual office of shepherd. For like a tree that has been planted in good earth, and, when it then grows a little, is moved away and planted in other, richer earth, so it happened to our father. Christ 25 planted him in Pbow. Afterwards he moved him away as we have said. He brought him north to this very mountain. So he came and found strength. His excellence reached up to heaven and his sweet savour to the end of the earth. But as weak eyes cannot bear the presence of

---

[115] I.e. ⲧⲟⲡⲟⲥ, "place".

[116] Cf. Constitutiones apostolorum VIII, 34, parts of 8-9, ed. F.X. FUNK, *Didascalia et Constitutiones Apostolorum* I (Paderborn, 1905), pp. 540-543; for a Sahidic version, see P. DE LAGARDE, *Aegyptiaca* (Göttingen, 1883), p. 284, Canones ecclesiastici, 75, parts of 39-40.

[117] Cf. *Dan.* 3.16ff.

[118] Cf. *Hebr.* 11.38.

[119] Cf. *Hebr.* 11.37.

[120] Cf. *Gen.* 31.3.

[121] *Is.* 25.10.

[122] Cf. *Ps.* 67.17.

[123] Cf. *Ps.* 131.14.

light, nor is there calm without waves[124], this is what happened
even to the holy apostles. So then when the enemy saw Apollo like a
vine in the desert, he gnashed his teeth and grew faint as he pondered
these thing deeply, saying : If Apollo watered the plant at the time
5   when Paul planted it, Christ made it grow so greatly[125]. If Apollo
brings his body as a plant to this mountain, how great is the extent
of its flowering! If this very grain of corn fills this land, it will yield
especially plentiful fruit. And when the enemy thought about these
things, he urged[126] his followers to wage war against this holy man.
10 * Again the latter-day Jebusites plotted to prevent the building of * p. 20
Zion[127]. Again the Philistines attempted to impede the settling of the
patriarch Isaac[128]; I am referring to the Meletians[129] who were present
in this mountain at that time, impeding by every means the settling
of this saint. And they said to one another : Let us afflict the righte-
15 ous man for he is inconvenient to us[130]. They gathered to him like
bees to a honeycomb[131]. But the man of God repelled them in the
name of the Lord like empty clouds blown along by winds[132], with
the prayers which he gives to him. Simply by the light of the Holy
Spirit in him those clouds passed before him and he then built his
20 holy place like the unicorn[133]. For the Holy Spirit likened this holy
community to the unicorn, that is the single horned one[134], that has
his horn straight up to heaven. Even if those that are brought forth
from it are many, still all the holy brethren of the community have
one single aim, that is the holy way of life, even if the good conduct
25 for which each one strives is different.

12. But let the matter and the community rest at this point, and
let us turn the flow of the discourse to him who was our founder
and forefather after Christ. Now our holy father * of whom we speak, * p. 21

---

[124] Lit. : "guidance"; I have emended the text.
[125] Cf. I *Cor.* 3.6.
[126] I have emended the tense of the verb.
[127] Cf. II *Kg.* 5.6 ff.
[128] Cf. *Gen.* 26.16 ff.
[129] On the continued existence of the Meletian sect, see H. I. BELL, *Jews and Christians
in Egypt* (London, 1924), pp. 42 f.; cf. also L. W. BARNARD, "Athanasius and the Meletian
Schism in Egypt", *Journal of Egyptian Archaeology* 59 (1973), pp. 181-189.
[130] Cf. *Is.* 3.10.
[131] Cf. *Ps.* 117.12.
[132] Cf. *Jude 12.*
[133] *Ps.* 77.69.
[134] I.e. μονόκερως.

when the Lord planted him in this mountain, then took root as Lebanon[135] and his branches went forth[136], that is the gifts of the Holy Spirit that are in him which I mentioned before : excellent fore-knowledge, marvellous vision, sound teaching, healing of the sick, so that the touching of only his garments gave them healing. There- 5 fore many came early in the morning to him to hear him[137] and to be healed of their diseases as (in the time) of Jesus, our God. And the effort of their zeal was not in vain for them. But the sick in body counted the healing of their pains as due to the grace of God who is with him. Moreover the sick in spirit he sent to the 10 harbour of repentance. Those in pains he comforted in their grief by giving them the remembrance of God, for it is he who administers all things to our profit. Those who had begun life he taught the way that leads up to the kingdom of heaven. Those who had grown in stature had their senses exercised[138] for the victory over the evil one. 15 Those whose fields were white[139], that is their grey hair of old age, he entreated to prepare themselves henceforth for their harvesting. And in brief[140], he helped everyone who went to him by the grace of the Holy Spirit that was in him. For such is the watering of Apollo[141] that those who give themselves as an offering to the Lord are added 20 to him daily[142], taking upon themselves the easy yoke[143] of the
* p. 22 excellent life. But the holy shepherd * received them most eagerly as gifts sent to him by the King of heaven. And he set himself up as an example for them in everything, in many fastings, in vigils often[144], so that he spent six years together without having gone in under a 25 roof to sleep at night, either in winter or in summer, as those who met him in person testified. It is plainly appropriate that he with the apostle should raise this very voice, saying : Our flesh did not receive any relief[145]. More particularly, when he saw the multitudes, he

---

[135] Or : "the frankincense-tree".
[136] Cf. *Hos.* 14.6-7.
[137] Cf. perhaps *Lk.* 21.38.
[138] Cf. *Hebr.* 5.14.
[139] Cf. *John* 4.35.
[140] Here the parallel text in Paris 129[13], 63 (Appendix I) begins.
[141] Cf. I *Cor.* 3.6.
[142] Cf. perhaps *Acts* 2.47.
[143] Cf. perhaps *Mt.* 11.29-30.
[144] Cf. II *Cor.* 11.27.
[145] II *Cor.* 7.5.

ascended the mountain[146]. That means that when the gathering of
the brethren who come to him took place through the Lord, he
ascended the pinnacle of the heavenly way of life. And he laid down
for them daily blessed promises in the age to come, if they fulfilled
5 in this age the promise of the philosophy according as they had
promised. He told them also that the falling away from their promise
is treachery. For then, said he, you have already given yourselves as an
offering to the Lord. It is not allowed to you henceforth to follow
the manner of life of the things belonging to the earth. This is a precept
10 of the Saviour who commands those who ascended to such a height
as this, by means of the symbol of the roof, not to come down to take
the things that are in the house[147], which are the carnal passions[148].

13. You have come out of the darkness of Egypt, and you have
come through the wave of the things which are like the disturbance
15 of the sea[149]. Beware, do not desire the passions of Egypt. You know
that when Israel ate of the corn of the land, they lost the * enjoyment   * p. 23
of the manna[150]. Do not, therefore, ask for things temporal[151] that
you may not lose the supper of the Lamb[152]. You have come out
from Sodom and you have gone far away from Zoar[153]. You have
20 ascended the spiritual mountain, which is the holy life. Beware, do not
abide in the tomb of pleasures, but, as if having advanced towards
the Lord, follow him without weariness. And even if you become
weary because of the weakness of nature, yet do not cast away your
patience which has great recompense of reward[154]. You have ad-
25 vanced to the vineyard of the King Christ. Be his workers who are
not ashamed, handling aright[155] the word of truth[156]. And do not ask
for the reward of your work until eventide, that is the end of your

---

[146] Cf. *Mt. 5.1.*

[147] Cf. *Mt. 24.17.*

[148] Here the parallel text in Paris 129[13], 63 (Appendix I) ends.

[149] Cf. *Ex. 14.*

[150] Cf. *Ex. 16.35.*

[151] Cf. perhaps II *Cor. 4.18.*

[152] Cf. *Rev. 19.9.*

[153] Cf. *Gen. 19.15*ff.

[154] Cf. *Hebr. 10.35.*

[155] ϣⲱⲱⲧ ⲉⲃⲟⲗ is difficult to render here, as it, in turn, translates ὀρθοτομέω
the meaning of which is in doubt, see G. KITTEL, *Theologisches Wörterbuch zum Neuen
Testament* VIII, pp. 112f., and the commentaries on II *Tim. 2.15.* Among the meanings
suggested the following two may be mentioned: "to expound rightly", "to follow
rightly".

[156] Cf. II *Tim. 2.15.*

days. For he that endures, he said, to the end, shall be saved[157],
said the Saviour. Remember always the progress of the incorporeal
powers whom the prophet Ezekiel saw going without turning backwards at all, not even with their faces[158]. In this way, O my sons, let
our race, too, be straight to heaven, as if we had laid upon our-   5
selves the yoke of salvation of our Saviour. Do not let demonic
plot, or bodily illness, or spiritual grief, or any other thing be able
to impede our zeal. But let us excel in the progress and the fore-
knowledge of virtue always, in order that also after the departure
from this prison we shall be in the choir[159] of those holy angels,   10
blessing the Lord with them for ever. And yet with other such words
* p. 24 did the saint * exhort the brethren day and night, exhorting them and
confirming them in the perseverance of perfection. Thus also his life
or his behaviour inspired them with zeal towards this. For the Preacher
often said about this: If the clouds be full of rain, they will empty   15
themselves upon the earth[160]. This means: If such exalted men be
full of the knowledge of heavenly things, they will dispense grace of
this kind to those who are disciples under them and those who follow
them always. And not those only but these others also who live in the
ways of this life received from his holy teaching. For our father is   20
truly a watchman of God who devoted himself to the salvation of
this generation. Therefore he laid down for them exhortations. For he
said to them as follows: Even if you will not be able to come up
to this spiritual mountain, which is this exalted life, nevertheless dwell
in purity in Zoar. Only do not stay in the neighbourhood of the men   25
of Sodom lest you receive of their blows[161]. And even if you have
traversed the sea of mankind and have come up into this wilderness,
into the land of promise that is in heaven, nevertheless do not let the
music of the sirens[162] that are in the sea beguile you, which are nine

---

[157] Cf. *Mt.* 10.*22*, 24.*13*; *Mk.* 13.*13*.

[158] Cf. *Ez.* 1.*9*, *17*; 10.*11*.

[159] The Greek word χορηγία is used in the text instead of χορός which one would
expect.

[160] *Eccles.* 11.*3*.

[161] Cf. *Gen.* 19.*15*ff.

[162] The sirens do not appear only in classical literature, but also in the Septuagint
(e.g. *Is.* 13.*21* etc.) and in Hellenistic Judaism. In the latter they are depicted as spirits of
the desert and companions of the demons (cf. PAULY-WISSOWA-KROLL, *Realencyklopädie
der klassischen Altertumswissenschaft* 3A (Stuttgart, 1929), p. 299b). I have not been
able to find any reference to their being nine in number.

destroyers [163]. The end of those, said the apostle, is death [164]. And
if it is a hard thing for you now to dwell in this very tent gladly [165]
like Joshua, the son of Nun [166], nevertheless follow the Lord with
all your heart like Caleb and go out to war and * return [167]. This means : * p. 25
5 Submit to the things that are fitting for the life without sin, that
you may inherit the heavenly land of the meek [168]. And even if you
will not dwell at the feet of the Lord in tranquillity like Mary, nevertheless refresh him bodily (through the poor) [169] like Martha [170], that
you, too, may be beloved of God. For Jesus, he said, loved Martha
10 and Mary, her sister [171]. And as a delightful torrent [172] gives its
enjoyment to all those who pass by it, so everyone who goes to this
saint receives from his marvellous teaching and from the grace of
the Holy Spirit that is in him. He had also been counted worthy at
that time of the dignity of the priesthood, for he attended the Lord
15 well without any distraction [173]. So also his throne was rightly prepared before the Lord. For the Lord God knows how to honour
those who honour him [174].

14. Moreover this very church, small as it is, in like manner he built
at that time, and the laity as well as the brethren urged him to conse-
20 crate it according to the canons. But he insisted that that should be
completed by the Lord. So on a day worthy of honour, which is the
25th of Epep [175], an angel of the Lord came to him. He said to him :
* Hasten to the service, for Christ calls you to that place. Now when * p. 26
the saint had entered the door, he raised his eyes and saw as it were
25 the ceiling of the church opened, and a multitude of the heavenly
host descending into it. Then when he looked at the table, he saw in a
wonderful vision the Lord standing upon it. And thus he completed

---

[163] The construction is obscure. It would seem that ⲛⲉⲧⲉⲣⲉ- is redundant.
[164] *Rom. 6.21.*
[165] Here the parallel text in Mich. 158/41 (Appendix II) begins.
[166] Cf. *Ex. 33.11.*
[167] Cf. *Josh. 14.11.*
[168] Cf. perhaps *Mt. 5.5.*
[169] The bracketed passage was added later in the text and is absent from the parallel
text.
[170] Cf. *Lk. 10.38-42.*
[171] Cf. *John 11.5.*
[172] Cf. *Ps. 35.9.*
[173] Cf. I *Cor. 7.35.*
[174] Cf. I *Kg. 2.30.*
[175] I.e. 19th July.

and consecrated it and celebrated communion in it. Therefore such a
high priest is ours who has so great a boldness before the Lord that
he sees things hidden and manifest. And of those who come to receive
of the holy mysteries, the Holy Spirit would reveal to him those who
are worthy and those who are not worthy. And as he knew them in   5
himself, the man of God would reveal it to the brethren to great
advantage. Many times, he said, when I was about to offer up the
holy, spiritual sacrifice[176], after I had broken that heavenly bread,
I would see each portion with the face perfect in them all[177]. And
when, he said, someone holy would come forward to communicate, 10
I would see them[178] running towards me, urging me to give to him.
But when, he said, someone unworthy would come forward to partake
of the holy mysteries, I would see them again withdrawing[179] to the
other side of the table, not wishing to be given to him. Therefore,
he said, when one of this sort came forward once to receive, I was 15
at a loss about this one. All the same I inclined towards charity.
* p. 27 And when I had given to him[180] the holy mystery, * I saw at once
one of the angels in attendance who took it from the man's hands
and put it once more upon the table. You have seen with what sort
of reverence and purity we shall be able to come forward to the 20
setting forth of the holy mysteries. And you, O man, who hears these
things, do not be unbelieving, but rather know from the purity of
this man. For unless he were perfect in all purity, he would have been
without vision. Besides, the holy apostle Paul appeared to him many
times, putting him right often. And he said to him : You have worked 25
at what is left (to do) of my ministry. Therefore to this day a cross is
erected in the place where he used to appear to him in the enclosure
(?)[181] which is at the south side of the church as proof[182] and
assurance for ever. Since I have recalled his vision, I shall not leave
out this other matter. For the tale is full of profit. It is grief yet full 30

---

[176] Cf. perhaps *Rom.* 12.1.

[177] The parallel text is to be preferred : "with the face of the Saviour perfect in them all".

[178] I.e. each portion of the Eucharistic bread.

[179] Reading with the parallel text ⲉⲅⲱⲗ for ⲉⲅⲱⲗⲙ.

[180] Here the parallel text in Mich. 158/41 (Appendix II) ends.

[181] The translation of ϩⲓⲣⲙⲟⲥ is doubtful. I have conjectured that ϩⲓⲣⲙⲟⲥ stands for εἱρμός which is derived from εἴρω "to fasten together", and is here perhaps used with the meaning of ὅρμος which is probably derived from the same verb. Alternatively, possibly emend ϩⲙⲡϩⲓⲣⲙⲟⲥ to read ϩⲛⲧⲉⲣⲏⲙⲟⲥ, "in the desert".

[182] Possibly : "complete proof".

of joy. It is encouragement for new plants; it is assurance for those
who stand firm.

15. For there was a brother among the brethren at that time, and
this man thought in his spirit of estrangement so as to become a
5 stranger to the brotherhood. By the providence of God another faithful man came to the gate, asking to be girded for the army of the
saints. O incomprehensible dispensation of God! O vision full of[183]
misery, O righteous judgement! For suddenly while they were still
troubled over the two destinies, this one asking to be taken in and
10 that one asking to desert, both were called forthwith out of this life
while they were still at the gates of their thoughts. However * this   * p. 28
matter was not hidden from our father, but rather he gathered together
the brethren and told them of the disposition of those who had fallen
asleep. And he testified to them through the Lord : Believe, O brethren,
15 that this faithful man who fell asleep was counted through the up-
rightness of his heart towards God in with the ranks of the holy
brethren, but that brother who died, as though estranged, because
of this became also a stranger to the crowns of his endurance. The
Lord said rightly : Watch, for you know not the day nor the hour[184].
20 For the recompense is according to free choice and according to
the perfection[185] of life, the life of each one. If someone is at a loss,
saying : Why did this man not die in the time of his virtue, I shall say :
Surely his former endurance also was hypocritical. For him who does
his works according to God, God never abandons. Let the great
25 David convince you who says : He shall never suffer the righteous to be
moved[186].

16. And again another time while he was standing at prayer at
night, he saw the devil in the guise that was written of him : walking
about, roaring like a lion[187]. And he put his nostrils on each one
30 of the brethren who were asleep as though sniffing at them (to find
out) whether his stench was in them. But when the holy shepherd,
the true guardian of the Lord's flock, had seen this one[188], he cried
out to him : O hard hearted one, unless my sons also give trouble

---

[183] If, as I have assumed, ⲑⲉⲣⲓⲁ stands for θεωρία, ⲉϥⲙⲉϩ should be emended
to read ⲉⲥⲙⲉϩ.
[184] *Mt. 25.13.*
[185] Or : "end".
[186] *Ps. 54.23.*
[187] Cf. I *Pet. 5.8.*
[188] I.e. the devil.

to you while they are asleep, unless they also persecute you by prayer, or shoot arrows at you by meditation[189], why do you not let them have their short sleep quietly? But that one answered : By your grey hairs, O Apollo, I do not molest them in any way now, but I marvel at them that they can bear to sleep at all while this great kingdom   5 is prepared for them. For, said he, if it were from me that repentance
* p. 29   was accepted even up to everything * that is grievous, I would not be (such) a thief. And the enemy said this as though advising for good, but because he is a mocker. For the enemy spoke and mocked the Lord. But the greatness of one[190] of the wonders of this righteous 10 man restrains[191] me not to set them forth. But again the word which is laid down for us requires me to leave their greatness behind. So angelic a man (was he) that the earth under his foot was equal (in power) to the prophets' words. For when he was passing by once with the brethren, a faithful man came forward in great faith. He gathered 15 a little earth from under the feet of the holy man. He took it and put it on his loaves of bread. And at once the container in which they were was filled up to the brim so that it overflowed on the ground. Is then this wonder smaller than those of the prophets? Even if you relate the blessing of the widow's handful of meal by Elijah[192], or the little 20 oil of the widow by Elisha the prophet[193], yet I say that these are not surpassing that which has been revealed now by our father. For those were sustainers only at the time of need by the prayer of the prophets when what was left over brought forth what was taken from it each time. But here without a word at all the earth under 25 his feet became like good leaven in the loaves of bread upon which it had been put and they became very plentiful, just as the Lord blessed them formerly in the desert[194]. And again when this torch-bearer of the Holy Spirit, our holy father Apa Apollo, came out once from the monastery, a woman with an issue of blood came forward to him in 30 firm faith. She touched the borders of his garments, and what had come to pass through our Saviour, he granted to his servant. At
* p. 30   once * when the woman touched the borders of his garments, the

---

[189] Or : "recitation (of the scriptures)".

[190] Assuming that ⲛⲟⲩ should be emended to read ⲛⲟⲩⲁ or ⲛⲟⲩⲉⲓ.

[191] ⲥⲉⲁⲙⲁϩⲧⲉ should be interpreted as *constructio ad sensum*, or should be emended to read ⲥⲁⲙⲁϩⲧⲉ.

[192] Cf. III *Kg.* 17.8-16.

[193] Cf. IV *Kg.* 4.1-7.

[194] Cf. *Mk.* 6.35-44 and parallels, and *Mk.* 8.1-10; *Mt.* 15.32-39.

fountain of blood stopped[195]. Then she departed, glorifying the Lord
and this saint Apa Apollo. For the Lord promised : He who believes
in me, the works that I do, he will also do, and he will exceed
them[196]. And again when he was once going to sail in a boat with the
5 brethren, and when we had departed to set sail[197], behold, a woman
ran out to him like the Canaanitish woman (did) formerly who is
written about in the gospels[198]. She cried out : Man of God, have
mercy on me. Remember me before the Lord that my earth may bring
forth human fruit, for she was barren. And[199] the holy man accepted
10 her faith and, as though fervent in the spirit[200], stretched forth his
hand and made the sign of the cross over the waters. He said to the
woman : Fill your hand and drink it in the name of the Lord, and go
in his faith. But she through the fervour of her heart did this twice.
And our father said to her : You will not be able to support these two
15 branches, my daughter. Then at the end of the next year[201] she was
found to be the mother of two sons. She sent them in to the holy man
that he should bless them as being the flowers of his prayers.

17. Moreover, many other things the man of God and true glorifier
of God, our father Apa Apollo, did. If I wish to tell these, one
20 by one, will my span of life let me relate them? Rather it is impossible
for me to tell them, even as it is an impossible thing for one to count
the stars and to number also * the rest of the things which God created. * p. 31
But is there any need to do this before you, before believing Christians?
These signs are for the unbelievers and not for those who believe,
25 as the great Paul said[202]. Moreover, this grace also God granted
to our blessed father by the perfection of his virtues so that he might
know the things that would happen before they did happen, and
also he saw the things that had happened in far off lands in the spirit
as if he, too, had the spirit of the prophets. And he related them to
30 those with him to the glory of God who revealed them to him. He
was also informed[203] at one time : It is necessary for the Patriarch

---

[195] Cf. *Mk. 5.25-34* and parallels.
[196] Cf. *John 14.12.*
[197] Cf. *Acts 21.1* (Sahidic).
[198] Cf. *Mt. 15.21-28*; (*Mk. 7.24-30*).
[199] Here the parallel text in BM Or. 3581 B(39) (Appendix III) begins.
[200] Cf. *Rom. 12.11.*
[201] Lit. : "the other year". The parallel text has "the year".
[202] Cf. I *Cor. 14.22.*
[203] Here the parallel text in BM Or. 3581 B(39) (Appendix III) ends.

Severus[204] to come and pray in your monastery. And this came to pass.
The light of Severus rose, and the righteous man was in another
district. The seer Samuel came and David was in the field[205]. Moses
sought after Aaron[206]. The Patriarch Severus came and the saint
Apa Apollo was in another district. So then this man prayed in the   5
habit of a stranger monk and went his way. Yet this was not hidden
from our father, but he at once went out to him. The saints know
the way of the saints. The great stags met one another[207], the likeness
of the prophets, the impress of the apostles. And the patriarch said to
our father: You are Apollo who is worthy of the joy of the saints.   10
Truly when I was in Antioch, I saw the light of your prayers and your
ascetic practices going to the high heaven, to the Lord, in glory. I then
* p. 32 went into * the wine-press of the righteous. And his fruits were going
to be in the wine-press of the righteous, being blessed of the Lord for
ever. When our father had prostrated himself at his holy feet and   15
besought him to return and spend the remainder of the day with him
in the monastery, the patriarch in turn besought (him), saying: The
time of my dissolution is at hand and I make haste to go that I may
reach my dwelling-place, the place where I shall lay down the burden
of my body. So then when they had saluted one another, this man   20
went his way, but our father returned to the monastery in great
gladness at having enjoyed the representative of Christ, the holy Severus.
I have advanced towards a great sea, which is the marvellous life of
this saint, this great luminary, and I do not know how I shall be
able to pass through the waves of his holy virtues. Therefore I shall   25
adopt the example of children who do not know how to swim. They
complete their enjoyment by the banks of the rivers. In similar manner
I too, since I am not able to reach the height of your[208] eulogies
which befit the perfection of the prophet, this apostle, this martyr, shall
therefore pass over or abandon the remainder of his marvellous works 30
and we shall come to the end of his blessedness in which he made
fast at the heavenly port. For if all measures are excellent before
God[209], according to the word of the wise Solomon, they are again

---

[204] A.D. 512-518 (died A.D. 538).
[205] Cf. I *Kg.* 16.*1-13*.
[206] Cf. *Ex.* 4.*14* ff.
[207] Cf. *Is.* 43.*15*.
[208] Probably read: "of the eulogies".
[209] Cf. *Prov.* 11.*1*, where the reference is to "the true measure".

entirely excellent before the men of God also. And that no one
should think that I was at a loss as to the honours that befit his
holiness, I fashioned the discourse in this way. What we have said
suffices for sensible believers as proof of the things I did not say.
5 In like manner I shall lay a trustworthy proof before those who think
in this way. So he who now wishes to know the magnitude of the
virtuous acts of our father in deed and not only in word, is enabled
* to apprehend these in part by what he sees. For if God is known by   * p. 33
his creatures, according to the word of the apostle[210], and if the tree
10 is known by its fruit[211], according to God's voice, and if, according
to the word of another wise man, man is known by his children[212],
then apprehend the greatness of Apollo by the fruits of his righteous-
ness. For if our father had not laboured, the Lord would not have
granted him this congregation worthy to be loved. Power of this sort
15 is manifest in the place where there are many children.

18. Lift up your eyes and see this angel-like camp, this host of
spiritual warriors, pursuing the hidden adversaries (?)[213]. They do not
sate their belly unreasonably, but as though reasonably, taking only
a little because of nature's need. Look at them casting down their
20 hidden adversaries (?)[214] through the breaking of the vessel, that is
the buffeting of the body[215], as the great Severus said, and (at) their
laying hold on that lamp of prudence, preparing themselves for the
meeting with the heavenly bridegroom[216]. For you will find among
these, old men who have trampled down the weakness of their grey
25 hair, running in the race[217] of virtue; young men who have vanquished
the evil one — such are they whom the crown of Christ leads on;
children who have grown up from being small in the purity of
the angels. If you have looked at these, turn * your face to the North   *p. 34
and look at this other convent which is not inferior to these people by
30 reason of the strength of virtue — I am speaking of the multitude

---

[210] Cf. *Rom.* 1.20.

[211] Cf. *Mt.* 12.33; *Lk.* 6.44.

[212] Cf. *Ecclus.* 11.28.

[213] I am not certain that I am correct in identifying the Greek loan-word in the
Coptic text as ἐναντιαῖος, or ἐναντίος.

[214] I am not certain that I am correct in identifying the Greek loan-word in the
Coptic text as ἀντίπαλος.

[215] Cf. perhaps I *Cor.* 9.27. — I cannot identify the quotation attributed to Severus
of Antioch.

[216] Cf. *Mt.* 25.1 ff.

[217] Cf. perhaps I *Cor.* 9.24.

of the wonders of those virgins who struggle to acquire for themselves the freedom from passion of the incorporeal beings. Look at
the multitude of the sacrifices which have gone to the Lord from his
two monasteries since the day when they were founded, most of all
the choir of the martyrs who became a burnt offering for the Lord, 5
being like costly precious stones in the midst of a beautiful crown.
So now you have known the greatness of him whom we honour. Now
you have seen the beauty of this spiritual tree that grew by the streams
of living waters[218], not having feared the scorching heat of the heretics
who came upon him, that brought its fruit in its season, that is in his 10
life. And also in God, he ceased bringing forth fruit by the grace of
him that sows the good seed, our Lord Jesus Christ[219]. For if he
promised this to the sons of Jonadab in the scriptures of old[220], how
much more will he do this for the children of grace at his coming.
So then even if we had not said anything at all in honour of our 15
father, the works would proclaim his excellence. For I did not write
these things as though telling you his life, since I am not fit for this
sort of undertaking, but I did this as though fulfilling the apostolic
command of him who says : Remember your great ones[221]. For he
whom we honour is truly great in heaven and upon earth. For there 20
is none greater than he that fears the Lord, as it is * written[222]. So
then he is very great indeed. Therefore the judge of the contest who is
in heaven, that is God, brought him into another great school of
virtues, that the excellence of him who bears the crown shall be
manifest as in the case of true athletes who keep adding to their 25
great contests. You have the proof of this from Paul and Job who
were victorious in such contests. So then do not be amazed when
you hear that the saints, too, were sick, but let Paul persuade you
when he says concerning himself and those like him in excellence :
Inasmuch as our outward man will perish, yet the inward man will be 30
renewed[223].

     19. This sort of pattern then was fulfilled in our father Apa Apollo,

*p. 35 (margin note at line 21)

---

[218] Cf. perhaps *Ps.* 1.3.
[219] Cf. *Mt.* 13.37.
[220] Cf. *Jer.* 42.18-19.
[221] *Hebr.* 13.7.
[222] *Ecclus.* 10.24, 25.10.
[223] Cf. II *Cor.* 4.16.

whether by the sufferings of asceticism or as a test for him from the
Lord. He fell into a great illness when his inward parts were stricken,
and thereafter he continued to spit blood and phlegm for the rest of
his days. So he was sick in this fashion, but his sickness was also a
5 healing for others. For while he was sitting one day speaking with
believers who had come to him to be blessed by him, there was one
among them, too, who was suffering from a sickness. O that spittle
that issued from the saint's mouth! O the sickness that became the
healer of another's sickness! For the sickness constrained our father
10 to expectorate such things. It is holy spittle, one might almost say.
At once when it had dropped upon the ground, the sick man took
it in perfect hope and swallowed it. And suddenly the grace of faith
became the healing of the believer through that holy spittle. And so
this man was healed, * but the saint continued in his sickness, indeed   * p. 36
15 the sickness became grievous to him, and henceforth he prepared
himself for the heavenly way. The brethren were grieved about him,
knowing that no one would be able to remedy the loss of such a father.
But the blessed father comforted the grief with the following words :
Why do you weep and put fearfulness into your own hearts? For
20 although my abiding in the flesh is needful for you, yet the departing
to be with the Lord is better for me[224]. For the dwelling-place of
those who rejoice is better than the dwelling-place of Kedar[225]. And
the land of the living[226] is better than the land of darkness and the
shadow of death[227]. Let not your heart be troubled, nor let it be
25 fearful[228]. For he who promised to be with us all the days even
unto the end of the world[229], that is God our Saviour, it is he who
shall prepare you, establish you, strengthen you, and give you a firm
foundation for ever[230], if only you yourselves abide in the laws and
your traditions which I established among you, which I, in my turn,
30 received through the laws of the first father of the community, Apa
Pachomius, which also the author of this new plant, the lawgiver
Apa Shenoute, confirmed. Before everything and above everything
keep the apostolic faith strictly without altering it in any way for the

[224] Cf. *Phil.* 1.*23-24*.
[225] Cf. *Ps.* 119.*5* etc.
[226] Cf. *Ps.* 26.*13* etc.
[227] Cf. *Is.* 9.*2* etc.
[228] *John* 14.27.
[229] Cf. *Mt.* 28.*20*.
[230] Cf. I *Pet.* 5.*10*.

sake of which I came to this place, and I shall also depart this life with
* p. 37 it intact by me. * For if you do these things, you will never fall[231].
But I, as though fighting in the good fight, I have finished the course
of the faith[232], and I have finished the work of the faith[233]. It
is better for me to go to him in whom I believe and to receive him   5
in perfection. Be strong and let your heart be assured and endure
in the Lord, knowing that he that endures to the end, the same shall
be saved[234], according to the Lord's promise. With these (words)
then and those like them the saint lightened the burden of the calamity
upon them because of him, while seeing that he was nigh to his   10
departure.

20. But before he died he bade them bring water to him. He washed
his face, his hands and his feet. He told them to pour it into the little
cistern on the south side. O how many healings came to pass in that
water which had received blessing! He also prayed over the gathering   15
of the holy community and over the bread and all the necessities
of the monastery. Then since everything that befits his perfection
was completed, he was placed on a certain day, on the 20th of the
month Paōne[235], in the temples of Christ, his King[236], to abide
before him for ever, to be made lord in his house, not over five or ten   20
cities only[237]. For this latter rule in their five cities belongs to those
who are saved apart, the natural and the corporeal, according to the
testimony of the store-house of all knowledge of the holy Severus[238].
But since our father for his part is the firstborn according to the grace
of the birth of the spirit and according to the calling of the saints of the   25
* p. 38 * fellowship, therefore also his dwelling-place is justly the heavenly
Jerusalem[239], the citadel and the brightest of all the cities that are in
heaven, whose builder and maker is God[240], in which there are ten
thousands of holy angels[239]; the joy of the righteous, the festival
assembly of the church of the firstborn who are enrolled in heaven[241],   30

[231] II *Pet.* 1.*10*.
[232] Cf. II *Tim.* 4.*7*.
[233] Cf. I *Thes.* 1.*3*; II *Thes.* 1.*11*.
[234] *Mt.* 10.*22*, 24.*13*; *Mk.* 13.*13*.
[235] I.e. 14th June.
[236] Cf. perhaps *Rev.* 3.*12*.
[237] Cf. *Lk.* 19.*17-19*.
[238] I cannot identify the quotation attributed to Severus of Antioch.
[239] Cf. *Hebr.* 12.*22*.
[240] Cf. *Hebr.* 11.*10*.
[241] Cf. *Hebr.* 12.*23*.

in which our father now enjoys the vision of the light of the holy
Trinity that is in unity. So now, O our father and guardian of souls,
since you have come to be among these and those like these, and
since you have entered that which is within the veil[242] to be our
5 ambassador before the Lord for ever, remember your community
which you have begotten from of old, this monastery in which you
dwelt. Take up on our behalf prayers and entreaties before him who
has power, Christ, in order that we, the sheep of your inheritance,
which dwell alone in the forest in the midst of Carmel[243], that is the
10 pure life, may attain all growth and all perfect progress until we all
come out of this marvellous tabernacle unto the house of God which
is more marvellous, the place where you are now with the Lord. But
now this people, orthodox and of the same belief, also themselves
ask the Lord that he should guard for them his peace that is full of
15 grace, and that he should feed them with all good things. This small
treatise that I have written in your memory, O our father, is very
insignificant in comparison with the greatness of the honours that
befit your all-holiness, even as the heaven is far distant from the earth.
But since to bless you, not only seven times a day * but all our life, is our   * p. 39
20 rightful debt, and also inasmuch as I know your condescension even
as you are a disciple of him who did not reject the two mites of the
widow[244], and the ointment of the woman of Bethany[245], and even
if my gift ... *2 lines missing* ... of their free [choice] ... the Lord [did not
reject.] Therefore, O our father, may my soul find favour before you,
25 but more especially, may you, Lord, be pleased with what I have
said. Grant sound vigour to those who love you and strengthen me,
too, by your blessing and your prayer, which shall be also our strength
and protection at our passing from you from this dwelling-place and
the passing of the river full of fear, until we arrive in the great light
30 that is above all, the light that does not set, impassable and im-
measurable, the holy Trinity that is in unity, the Almighty, the Word,
the Paraclete, to whose lordship is due all glory, all worship and all
thanks, not only from us men but also from the host that is above
the world, now and always, for ever and ever. Amen.

[242] Cf. *Hebr. 6.19.*
[243] Cf. *Mic. 7.14.*
[244] Cf. *Mk. 12.42-44; Lk. 21.2-4.*
[245] Cf. *Mt. 26.6ff.; Mk. 14.3ff.*

APPENDIX I

Paris 129¹³,63

*p. 40 (12.) * In brief, he helped [every]one who went to him by the grace
of the Holy Spirit that was in him. For such is the watering of Apollo[1]
that those who give themselves as an offering to the Lord are added 5
to him daily[2], being delivered from the heavy yoke, while he puts upon
them the easy yoke[3], which is the pure life. But the holy shepherd
received them very eagerly as gifts sent to him by the King of heaven.
And he set himself up as an example for them in everything, in many
fastings, in vigils often[4], so that he spent six years together without 10
having gone in under a roof to sleep at night, either in winter or in
summer, as those who met him in person testified. As for that man's
voice (it is appropriate)[5] that he with the apostle should raise it,
*p. 41 saying : Our flesh did not [receive relief][6]. * Especially when he saw the
multitudes, he ascended the mountain even more[7]. That means that 15
when the brethren gathered unto him through the Lord, he ascended
the pinnacle of the heavenly way of life. And he laid down for them
daily blessed promises in the age to come, if they fulfilled in this age
the promise of the philosophy according as they had promised. And
he told them that the falling away from their promise is treachery. 20
For now, said he, you have already given yourselves as an offering
to the Lord. It is not allowed to you henceforth to follow the manner
of life of the things belonging to the earth. For this is a precept of our
Saviour who commands those who ascended to such a height, by
means of the symbol of the roof, not to come down to take the things 25
that are in their house[8], which are the carnal passions.

---

[1] Cf. I *Cor. 3.6.*
[2] Cf. perhaps *Acts 2.47.*
[3] Cf. perhaps *Mt. 11.29-30.*
[4] Cf. II *Cor. 11.27.*
[5] The bracketed passage is supplied from the parallel text.
[6] Cf. II *Cor. 7.5.*
[7] Cf. *Mt. 5.1.*
[8] Cf. *Mt. 24.17.*

APPENDIX II

Michigan 158/41

(13.) * in purity like Joshua, < the son of > Nun[1], nevertheless follow * p. 43
the Lord with all your heart like Caleb and go out to war and return[2].
5 This means: Submit to the things that are fitting for the life without
sin, that you may inherit the heavenly land of the meek[3]. And even if
you will not dwell in tranquillity at the feet of the Lord like Mary,
nevertheless refresh him bo[dily] like [Mar]tha[4], that [you, too, may]
be beloved of God. For Jesus loved Mary and Martha, her sister[5].
10 And as a delightful torrent[6] gives its enjoyment to all those who pass
by it, so everyone who goes to this saint receives from his marvellous
teaching and from the grace of the Holy Spirit that is in him. He had
[also] been counted worthy at that [time * of the] dignity [of the] priest- * p. 44
hood, for [he] attended the Lord well without distraction[7]. So also
15 his throne was rightly prepared before the Lord. For God knows how
to honour those who honour him[8].

14. Moreover this church, small as it is, in like manner he built at
that time, and the brethren and the laity urged him to consecrate it
according to the canons. But he insisted that that should be completed
20 by the Lord. So on a day worthy of honour, which is the 25th of Epep[9],
an angel of the Lord came to him. He said: Apollo, hasten to the
service, for Christ calls you to that place. Now when the saint had
entered the door, he saw as it were the ceiling of the church opened,
and a multitude of the * heavenly host descending upon it. So then * p. 45
25 when he looked round at the table, he saw the Lord standing beside
him[10] in a wonderful appearance. And thus he completed and consecrated it according to the holy canons. Therefore we have such a high

[1] Cf. *Ex.* 33.*11*.
[2] *Josh.* 14.*11*.
[3] Cf. perhaps *Mt.* 5.*5*.
[4] Cf. *Lk.* 10.*38-42*.
[5] Cf. *John* 11.*5*.
[6] Cf. *Ps.* 35.*9*.
[7] Cf. I *Cor.* 7.*35*.
[8] Cf. I *Kg.* 2.*30*.
[9] I.e. 19th July.
[10] The parallel text has "upon it" (the table), a reading to be preferred.

priest who has boldness before the [Lord] to see things hidden and
manifest. And of those who come to receive of the holy mysteries,
the Spirit would reveal to him those who are worthy and those who
are not worthy. And as the man of God knew them in himself, he
would reveal it to the brethren to their great advantage. For many   5
times, he said, when offering [up the] holy sacrifice, after I had broken
that heavenly bread, I would see each portion with the face of the
* p. 46 Saviour perfect in * them all. And when, he said, someone holy would
come forward to receive, I would see them[11] as though running
towards me, urging me to give to him. But when, he said, someone 10
defiled would come forward to partake, I would see them as though
withdrawing to the other side of the table, not wishing to be given
to him. Therefore, he said, when one of this sort came forward once
to receive, I was at a loss about this one. All the same[12] I inclined
towards charity. And when I had given to him   15

---

[11] I.e. each portion of the Eucharistic bread.
[12] Lit.: "Likewise" (ϩομλιωс = ὁμοίως), but I suspect it stands for ὅμως, particularly as the Morgan text reads ϩωμωс.

APPENDIX III

BM Or. 3581 B(39)

(16.) * And the holy man, Apa Apollo, accepted her faith and, as though   * p. 47
fervent in the spirit[1], stretched forth his hand and made the sign of
5 the cross over the waters. He said to the woman : Fill your hand and
drink it in the name of the Lord, and go in [his] faith. But she
through the fervour of her heart did this twice. And our holy father
said to [her : Will] you be able to support these two [bran]ches, [my]
daughter? Then at [the] end of the year [she] was found to be the mother
10 of two sons. She sent them in to the holy man that he should bless
them as being the flowers of his prayers.

    17. Moreover, many other things the man of God and true glorifier
of God, our father Apa Apollo, did. If we are to tell them, one by
one, will [my] span of life let [me] relate them? Rather it is impossible
15 for me to tell them, even as it is an * impossible thing for one to count   * p. 48
the clouds or to number also the rest of the things which God created.
But neither is there the need to do this before you, believing Christians.
For the signs are not for those who believe, as the great Paul said[2].
Moreover this grace also the Lord granted to our blessed father by
20 the perfection of his virtues so that he might know the things that
would happen before they did happen as if he, too, had the spirit
of the prophets, and he saw the things that had happened in far off
lands in the [spirit]. And to those with him he told them, as though
they were present at them, to the glory of the Lord who revealed
25 [them] to him. [He] was [also in]formed

---

[1] Cf. *Rom.* 12.*11*.
[2] Cf. I *Cor.* 14.*22*.

INDEX OF REFERENCES AND CITATIONS

A. BIBLICAL

B. OTHERS

INDEX OF PROPER NAMES

INDEX OF SUBJECTS IN M579

Prophet (O.T.): 4,*1,30*; 5,*4*; 7,*28*; 8,*1*ff.; 11,*13*ff.; 18,*3*; 22,*14*ff.; 23,*29*. — of Apollo : 1,*4,11*; 2,*17*; 7,*20*; 24,*29*.

Quaternity, describing Chalcedonian "heresy" : 12,*15*.

Severus, Apollo's meeting with : 23-24. — journeyings of : 12,*27*ff.
Sirens : 18,*29*.

Trinity : 29,*31*. — Trinitarian controversy : 11-12.
Troubles in monasteries, especially Pbow : 2,*30*ff.; 12-14.

Vigils : 7,*5,21*; 16,*24*.
Virgins : 26,*1*.
Visions : 6,*18*; 7,*28*ff.; 9,*9*ff.; 19,*22*ff.

CONTENTS

Imprimerie Orientaliste, s.p.r.l., Louvain (Belgique)